Wrong Side of History

AMERICA'S ALLIANCE WITH ISLAMIC TERRORISTS

SARAH WESTALL

Wrong Side of History

To the millions who have died for their country

CONTENTS

ACKNOWLEDGMENTS

Special thanks to Senator Richard Black for his
extraordinary commitment to our country and for his
compassion to the people of Syria.

INTRODUCTION

The escalation of tensions and conflict with Syria,
Russia, and North Korea is troubling. Especially in a
world where nuclear weapons and other mass killing
devices are capable by all sides. It cannot be
understated how serious actions of the United States are
in the eyes of the world and what the ramifications of
those actions could be.

With this in mind, I invited Senator Richard Black to
my radio show, Business Game Changers, to discuss
these issues. He has a unique perspective on the United
States involvement in the Middle East, with NATO, and
with Russia. His vast experience in the military, as well

as his time at the pentagon as head of the Army's Criminal Law Division, provides him with incredible knowledge on these issues.

What you will not hear in the media, which will be shared with you in this book, is that the United States has formed an unwritten alliance with Saudi Arabia, Qatar, and Turkey to take out Assad, the president of Syria. These three regimes are some of the most brutal, oppressive regimes that have ever existed in human history. It is well documented that they all have brutal dictatorships with aggressively oppressive governments. On the other hand, Syria, before the war, was one of the five safest countries on Earth. They believed in equal rights for women and people of all religions practiced peacefully side by side.

Senator Richard Black has studied Syria every day for the past 7 years. With his experience in the Middle East, as well as his day to day studies, he felt compelled in 2014 to write a letter directly to President Assad. The complete details of that letter is included in this book along with Senator Black's own words as to why he wrote the letter and what he hoped would come out of it.

Not long after the letter was sent, President Assad reached out to Senator Black and invited him to visit the country. Consequently, Black went on a 3-day visit to meet and to talk with President Assad directly in Syria. You will learn what happened during that trip to Syria and what Senator Black learned about the country and about both Bashar al Assad and his wife Asma Assad.

Senator Black also shares many other insights about the Middle East, Syria, Russia, and the wealthy oligarchs that control the United States, NATO, and most of the world. You will hear that if Assad falls, over 4 million innocent people will be slaughtered; including 2 million Christians, 2 million Shiites (moderates who support Christians), moderate rebels, Jews in the region, and many other groups. Black believes that "it will be one of the worst slaughters in human history".

You will also learn how and why tensions between Russia and the United States have escalated unnecessarily and have become very serious. He shares the downward path NATO has been on for the last three decades; from a defensive peace coalition to a brutal organization that continues war for its own survival.

This information is not readily available in the main stream media. Please share with your family and friends the important information that is contain in these pages. We do not want to be on the wrong side of history any longer.

Note: On several occasions throughout the interview, Al Qaeda and 911 are mentioned. I want to make a point that I believe that the United States official version about the events on 911 is highly suspect, if not completely false. Regardless of your views on who is to blame for 911, Al Qaeda is a brutal terrorist organization and is the group that the United States officially blamed for the murder of over 3000 U.S. citizens on that day. It is unfathomable that the United States could align themselves with the same organization that they have blamed for murdering 3000 of our own people.

INTERVIEW TRANSCRIPT

Senator Richard Black's Official Transcript from Business Game Changers Radio Interview with Sarah Westall on 5/3/17

Westall:

Hi Senator Black welcome to the program.

Black:

I am delighted to be with you. I appreciate you having me on today

Westall:

Well, I am really glad that you decided to come because I really want to hear your thoughts on a lot of things that are going on around the world. But before we get into this, I want people to realize what your background is because it is really quite significant. Other than being a state senator right now, you also have extensive military service. You were in 269 combat missions in Vietnam, and then you worked your way up to the Chief of the Criminal Law Division at the Pentagon. Can you tell us a little bit about your background going all the way up to your latest position?

Black:

Yes, and mostly, I like people to understand, I don't come at this from your typical antiwar activist. My radio network was killed right beside me while we were attacking enemy positions on the ground while I was a forward air controller. But, before that I fought as a Marine Helicopter pilot, some of the most heated battles that we had ever since the 2nd World War. And then later I went on and went back to school. Later, I went back to Law School and I entered the Army JAG corp. I was a career prosecutor. I think in a very logical structured way as a prosecutor does. Something I should mention... Now in-between, I was over in Europe during the Cold War. I was part of the NATO forces, although I consider myself an American soldier, not a NATO solider. But I was part of NATO at a time when NATO was a fine organization. It was a defensive alliance and I don't think it is today, but it was then. And so, one of the jobs I had, I was in charge of military justice for all of the Middle East and North Africa. So I had responsibilities, I dealt with Saudi Arabia, I dealt with Egypt and this sort of thing. And, I got involved really, sort of re-involved, in the Middle East because I had interest in foreign affairs since I was a child, literally. And it has been very intense at various times.

And I started looking at what we are doing in Libya. I thought this must have to do with oil and I looked into it. It really did not have too much to do with oil as it did with capturing the weapons from Libya. Now there were a couple of reasons, like most wars, there is not just one reason. One of the big reasons was to capture their huge arsenal of weapons and use it to overthrow the government of Syria. That really was the genesis of my interest in Syria. I didn't know a lot about Syria before that. I didn't understand it, but all of a sudden it became enormously important. I have followed the Syrian war and learned the Syrian culture and history and so forth over a period of six years. There virtually hasn't been a day where I did not take some time out to pay attention to what was going on in Syria. So, that is a little bit of my background. I had a pretty strange upbringing and so I have a very wide range of experiences that most political figures don't have.

Westall:

So when you were the Chief of the Criminal Law Division at the Pentagon, what kinds of things did you do that got you involved? You said you worked primarily with Africa and the Middle East. So what typical things would you have done?

Black:

Now, at the Pentagon I was the Head of the Criminal Law Division and we prepared legislation that was enacted by congress. Each year we would prepare an executive order that went to the president of the United States for signature. I testified before congress on a number of occasions. So I am intimately familiar with the inner workings of the Pentagon and the way the executive and the judicial and the legislative branches all interface. It was an excellent background and one that is rather rare. You don't have many people who have worked in all 3 branches of government and who have worked both at the federal and state level. So that is my background.

Westall:

So you did an interesting thing last year; you wrote a letter to Assad. First of all, what was the point of that letter, what was in it?

Black:

I wrote the letter to President Assad and I thanked him
for the Syrian Arab armies gallant campaign that they
waged on the Qalamoun mountain range. This is the

Senator Black Letter to Assad (below is full text)

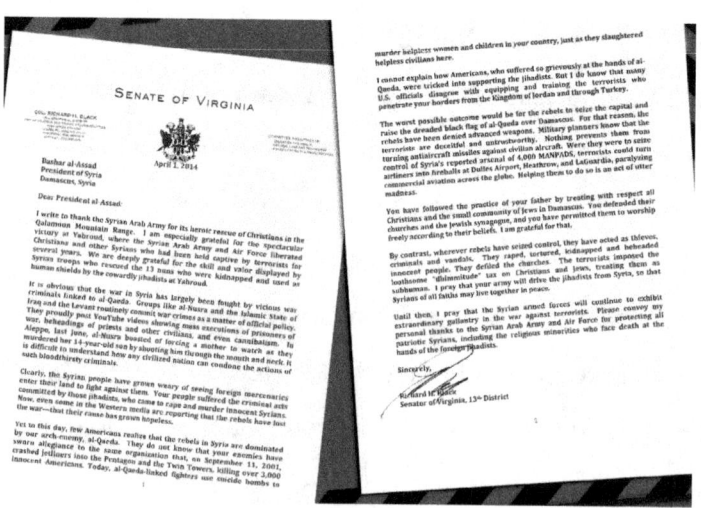

mountain range that separates Lebanon and Syria. The
terrorists had taken control of that whole mountain
range and there are many Christian villages there. Many

of them still speak the original language of Jesus Christ, which is Aramaic. There were slaughters taking place of the Christians and the Alawites, who are known as the friends of the Christians. So the Syrian army, you know, we could do a complete article or report on this. They did a magnificent, heroic counter attack, a campaign and eventually they recaptured 13 nuns; catholic nuns who were being used as human shields. So I wrote, "I want to thank you for rescuing the Christians on the Qalamoun mountain range". But in my heart, I wasn't speaking only about Christians, although I am a very committed Christian, but I hate to see innocent people being slaughtered. This is really where I am coming from. I fought on the ground in Vietnam and in the air. Often I supervised prisoners who were recently captured on the battlefield. I treated them with respect, dignity, and kindness. As long as they were out of the war, they were going to be treated well when they were under me. I don't have an innate hatred of people just because they are from a different culture or different religion or whatever. So I wrote the letter to President Assad and I thanked him for that. I thanked him for the fact that both he and his father before him had been protectors of the Christians and other religious minorities in Syria. And finally I told him, I cannot explain to you why the United States, which lost 3000 people to Al Qaeda when they brought down the twin towers and crashed into the Pentagon on 911. I cannot explain to you why the United States has formed an alliance with Al Qaeda. And those were the messages that I sent to him.

The Nov 14th 2015 letter follows:

Bashar al Assad President of Syria, Damascus, Syria.

Dear Mr. President:

I was pleased by the Russians' intervention against the armies invading Syria. With their support, the Syrian army has made dramatic strides against the terrorists.

I was delighted by Syria's resounding victory over ISIS at the Kuwairis Airfield. My compliments to those who heroically rescued 1,000 brave Syrian soldiers from certain death. I am convinced that many such victories lie ahead.

The Syrian War was not caused by domestic unrest. It was an unlawful war of aggression by foreign powers determined to force a puppet regime on Syria. General Wesley Clark, former Supreme Allied Commander Europe, revealed that by 2001, Western powers had developed plans to overthrow Syria. Yet after fifteen years of military subversion, NATO, Saudi Arabia and Qatar still cannot identify a single rebel leader who enjoys popular support among the Syrian people.

Foreign powers have no right to overturn legitimate elections and impose their will on the Syrian people. Syrians alone must determine their destiny, free of foreign intervention. I am disappointed that the UN has turned a blind eye to the unlawful interference in Syria's internal affairs.

Before the war began, Syrians had the greatest religious freedom and women's equality of any Arab people. Many Americans are surprised to learn that the Syrian Constitution provides for free elections, religious freedom, women's rights, and the Rule of Law. Before criticizing Syria, the U.S. might first insist that our allies Jordan, Saudi Arabia, Qatar, UAE and Kuwait grant similar freedoms to their own people.

I am disappointed that the U.S. has countered Russian assistance to Syria by forwarding shipments of TOW anti-tank missiles to the terrorists. This will only prolong bloodshed in Syria. And supplying weapons to "good terrorists" while denying them to "bad terrorists" is a fool's game. The reckless dissemination of TOW missiles threatens worldwide civil aviation. Long-range anti-tank weapons can easily be targeted to destroy passenger jets taxiing for takeoff. As a Virginia Senator, I am concerned that such missiles might find their way to remote areas adjacent to Reagan National Airport, Dulles International Airport and others. I have corresponded with the United States President about these concerns.

Today, the Army of Conquest receives extensive U.S. military support. The Army of Conquest is formed around al Nusra, which has sworn allegiance to al Qaeda. This means that the U.S. supplies weapons to the same terrorists who murdered 3,000 Americans on 9-11. This is an obscene betrayal of the victims of 9-11.

People have begun realizing that the Syrian terrorists are militarily supported by our allies, Turkey, Saudi Arabia, and Qatar. Indeed, ISIS has no more loyal backer than Turkey, which serves as its main conduit for jihadists, weapons, medical support and trade.

Although Turkey is included in the Coalition against ISIS, it has contributed nothing of significance toward the Coalition's lackluster performance.

It is apparent that the objective of the Turks and Saudis is to impose a murderous theocratic dictatorship on the Syrian people. If they succeed, Christians and other minorities will be slaughtered or sold into slavery. Many good-hearted Sunni and Shia Muslims will also be burned, drowned, crucified and beheaded.

But world opinion is turning against the terrorists and their supporters. The cruel mistreatment of captured Syrian soldiers by terrorist's groups is appalling. Many Americans find the behavior of these so-called "moderates" morally abhorrent.

I bled, fighting to defend this nation's honor. I will oppose American support for terrorists, like the Army of Conquest and ISIS that threaten Syria. Many

Virginians join in praying that the Syrian Arab Army and its allies will triumph over the forces of evil, and that peace will soon return to Syria

Thank you for protecting the lives of Christians and of all good people of Syria.

Sincerely, Richard H. Black Senator of Virginia, 13th District.

Westall:

So he [Assad] ended up inviting you to a meeting and you went April of last year. What occurred at that meeting and what did you learn about him?

Black:

First of all, keep in mind that by that time I have spent 5 years studying the war. I had studied him and I had studied his wife. accessible on the internet and you can listen to the things that they say. People don't

Senator Black visiting Assad in 2016

understand; they just say "there is this tyrant over there". But Assad never wanted to be the president of Syria. His brother was being groomed, and all of a sudden his brother was killed in an accident. Assad was a young man who had fallen deeply in love with a Syrian American who was raised in London. A fantastic woman, a women of enormous intellect. The two of them are extremely intelligent. He is a modest soft spoken man. He has a very precise logic. He is highly intelligent. And his wife, interestingly, she has this off the Richter scale intelligence and intellect. But, she is very humble. She wears no jewelry. If she showed up next to you at the meat counter at the grocery store and you dropped something, she would be the first one to pick it up and say here you are. There is also sort of a charismatic glow about her. Now she is more, sort of, the difference between men and women I suppose. She

Asma Assad

does sort of exudes a certain excitement and so forth. But you can tell when the two of them are together they are deeply in love. They are young people. When she speaks I notice the body language. She folds his hands and he listens to her. You can just sense the tremendous affection. And he said you know, they have two children, when my children say "when daddy your there, you are the president. But when you are home, mama is the president". You can just see these interactions between the two of them. Asma Assad is an extremely accomplished woman. She has told me that she has visited over 1000 families who have had sons who had killed in the war. She said she was apprehensive at first when she went because she thought, "you know they were going to be distraught, they are going to be screaming and yelling" and so forth. She said, "it has never happened". She said, "in virtually every case, despite the tragedy they have been through, they are all very proud that their sons, if they had to die that they died in the defense of Syria". It has been a very humbling experience for her. She is very

genuine. You cannot speak with her without
understanding that you are not getting a political
diatribe. Just on a side, I personally know an individual
who owned an apartment in Damascus. When the
Assad's first moved in, when he was going to become
the president of Syria, one day this fellow said, my
neighbor said "do you know who just moved in? It's
president Assad and their children". They didn't move
to some palace. You have the Turkish president,
Erdogan, who built himself a 1000 room palace; 21
times the size of the White House. President Assad
moved into an ordinary apartment with people. He
drove himself in the SUV; he didn't have a driver. He
maintains relatively light security, which makes me
nervous. But, he feels confident among the Syrians. The
Syrians love him. They adore the Assad's despite what
you hear. And he feels safe. Now, he's got to show up
unannounced because he has the CIA, he's got Mossad,
he's got MI6, MIT, French Intelligence, everybody,
Saudi Arabia, the whole bunch of them. Everybody is
out to kill him.

Westall:

Why?

Black:

Because they understand. It's for the same reason that you continue to hear them say, "Assad must go. Assad has to leave". They recognize that Assad is the glue that holds the nation together. The people of Syria, now I am not saying everybody, but the Syrians, absolutely have a heartfelt love for the first family. And, the Syrian army likewise feels this loyalty to him. And the people feel the loyalty to the army. I heard it described as a 3 strand robe that is all woven together; the president, the army, the people. If you look at it, going back into history, ancient history now, when Adolf Hitler headed Germany, he had immense supporters, he must have had a dozen attempts on his life; some of them extremely serious. There has not been an assassination attempt on Assad in 6 years of war. Over 6 years, the army has been loyal. He says repeatedly, "look, if the Syrian people or the army wanted me gone, a group of soldiers could march in here any day and say, you're out of here".

Westall:
Because it's easy, he doesn't have a ton of security

Black:
He doesn't, it's remarkable.

Westall:
So this latest chemical attack, it seems coming from what you are saying now, it seems almost impossible that a person like that would do a chemical attack against his own people without his own people rebelling against him.

Black:
It is a fake. You know it has happened twice. It happened in 2013 with the gas attacks in the Gouda suburb of Damascus. That was the very famous red line attack. Now you have the Ka Sukoon attack. Now, I am

an attorney so I tend to think logically. Ok, what do you have to prove before you go to the jury. Well, the first thing that you always want to prove is "what is the motive". Ok, we believe this man killed his wife because just two months before he took out a huge insurance policy on his life... da da da. You list all of these things. So I defy anyone in the federal government or in think tanks, anyone to explain and to give me a motive why president Bashar al-Assad of Syria would launch an attack on a random group of civilians overlooking the tremendous battles that he is fighting. Why do you launch sarin gas on people with baby strollers instead of terrorist driving tanks? It makes no sense, it's irrational.

Westall:

There was no strategic thing, there wasn't anyone who was trying to target in that group. Plus, the people love him, if he had any pattern of behavior like that they would not like him.

Black:

No, and think about this also. This is one of the things that really troubles me because I am a Trump supporter and I am watching what is going on with foreign policy and there has been some very grave disappointments. On the 30th of March, there were 3 people who came out and said we no longer intend to topple Assad; Sean Spicer said it, Nikki Haley said it, and Rex Tillerson. So we had very prominent people. Now, it's just days after that, on the 4th of April, the terrorists in Ka Sukoon published a whole series of videos that were produced by the Aleppo Media Center. Now the Aleppo Media Center is a propaganda center that is run by terrorists allied with Al Qaeda, the groups that brought down the twin towers. This was the principle evidence that was used by the United States in coming to a conclusion that we had to attack Syria. What was it that caused us to find credibility? This was like in the 2nd world war if Adolf Hitler had said "hey look, look at what has happened over here" and we immediately say "oh my gosh, we have to change the direction of the war because Adolf Hitler has sent these videos to us". The videos came from Al Qaeda or people who were allied with Al Qaeda. I look at the timeline, 3 days from the time that we get these videos from the terrorists, we analyze them, we conclude that it must have been Syria and not the people who sent the videos. We convene a meeting of the National Security Council. They determine that we have to take action, we select a target. The Pentagon sends out orders, we move guided missile cruisers into position and we fire the missiles onto the target. All of that takes place in a span of 3 days.

Westall:

So you know that they were planning it. This is what you are saying?

Black:

I've got to tell you. I have been around the Pentagon for a long time. Remember how long it took us to react from Benghazi? I mean, two weeks later we were still in utter chaos. I am not saying that the Pentagon isn't better run, but it's not that well run. I have been in the Pentagon; I know how things go. It goes systematically. You cannot analyze the intelligence, let alone set in action all of these things in a 3-day span. It is very suspicious the fact that we basically changed American policy. We said, we are no longer going to get rid of Assad. That was a game changer. For Assad, that was the predicate for winning the war. If you know you are going to win the war, why would you suddenly go out and provoke the United States with a gas attack that you have agreed to by treaty that you would never do?

Westall:

It doesn't fit his pattern of behavior. Could there be someone in his inner circle or someone around him that could have done that? It may not have come from him, but someone in his government?

Black:

I don't believe so. The Syrian Army is very very
structured. It is an extremely professional army. Now
they have militias and so forth. But the militias would
have no access to this. Remember, we were the ones
who said that he had no more sarin gas; he agreed to
turn over. I don't discount the fact that it is conceivable
that somebody withheld something or that something
was overlooked and there is something out there. But
we know from intelligence, from the 2013 attacks, that
there were a number of commanders asking President
Assad to release sarin gas. We know it because they
had a lot of sarin gas at the time. Each and every time
he refused to do it. So it is clearly something he is in
control of.

Westall:

Wouldn't you say that if a renegade in his government
somewhere did it, that it wouldn't be a reason to go to
war or to blast him, because he wouldn't be happy
about it either. It would be like somebody, a renegade,

doing something against the government, it doesn't mean the government did it.

Black:

No, and if you think of it... Let's say there was someone out there. Let's say there was a general in some fantastical difficult battle and he somehow got hold of this. Who would he attack? Would he attack waves of Islamic jihadist with tanks, who have slaughtered all of his men? Or would he say, "wow I just found a couple of chemical shells, let's go ahead and let's send them and shoot some people who are walking down the street".

Westall:

It makes no sense. So why do you think Trump did this? Probably you have been thinking about that a lot. Why would Trump do this after all of his election rhetoric, why would he do this?

Black:

I have thought about it a lot. Now I am getting into speculation and I like to distinguish between where I am talking about things I know with absolute certainty. I know with absolute certainty that Syria did not launch that gas. I can say that because, as a prosecutor, if I had one of my trial counsel who said "there is absolutely no motive for this, but we are going to go ahead and try it anyway" I would say, "get out of here, we have better things to do".

Westall:

So why didn't Trump say, we have better things to do?

Black:

No jury in the world is ever going to convict somebody with no motive. It doesn't happen. But I did look. So what is the motive for setting up this very peculiar and very short timeline? I can only speculate. But I know that the democrats have made a huge thing of this alleged Russian hacking and the media played along with it. There is absolutely no evidence to support it, but they just went on and on. And after a while, it was Herman Goebbels, the great NAZI propagandist who said "if you just repeat it over and over people will believe it no matter what it is". So, I think to some extent he said "look, if we can take that off the headlines, let's do it". If you look at the way we structured the strike on the air field, we fired 59 missiles, I think all but about 10 of them either miss fired or missed their targets. These are pretty accurate missiles. A lot of them missed and the others did very minor damage. But at the same time, it did manage to suddenly, it took Russia out of the headlines. So, people in the Presidency do things because sometimes they have to do them. To me that's kind of the best scenario. I don't for a moment believe that somebody rushed into his room and said "oh look, here is a picture of a dead Syrian child".

Westall:

His daughter crying [sarcasm]

Black:

Give me a break. I have looked at a thousand beheadings. Literally, I am not exaggerating. A thousand beheadings of Christians, of Alawites, of Shiites, of all of these people. If somebody shows me a picture of a little girl; I have a lot of little girls in my family, I love them dearly, but it's not going to cause me to change my position. I don't believe that is what happened. I think that was sort of a, you know, kind of a throw away. So, that is disturbing. It takes us into the issue of what is happening with the Trump foreign policy. If you look at the foreign policy, that was a constant throughout his campaign, he was going to improve his relations with Russia, he was going to down grade his relations with NATO, because it has become outmoded. He was going to stop this irrational war against Syria and focus on the terrorists. In each of those areas he has retracted his position. I would tell you as a military person, I was prepared to die fighting against the Soviet Union. I spent 3 years in Germany. I used to trudge along, at 2, 3 in the morning in our little village thinking about, would I be able to get the family out on one of the first planes before I went to the front and died? Because that was our job. We were supposed to hold the line until reinforcements would come from the United States. I was a great believer in NATO, but I have watched NATO. When the Berlin wall fell, we made a firm commitment, the Secretary of State of the United States and the Foreign Minister of Germany said, "we will not move NATO one inch towards Russia". The beauty of it was that suddenly we went from being toe to toe with the Soviet Union, two nuclear powers where anything could trigger a worldwide confrontation, and all of a sudden we had a thousand miles of separation. That gave us time if there was something that flared up; we had a hotline. The presidents could get on a hotline, say "you know we just saw a missile go off". "Yah I know you saw that. This is some whacky thing that just went wild. Don't worry about. We are going to explode it when it gets up to here." "Ok, we will just watch and see". Now we have moved closer and closer. We have violated the agreement with the Soviet Union and now we literally have battalions of American troops on the Russian border.

Westall:

Why? Because they are a nuclear power, we are a nuclear power; why would we not want to maintain as much as a friendly, peaceful situation with something that is so potentially terrible? You know, nuclear war is off the charts.

Black:

It is, and if you look at the major disagreements we have with Russia, we disagree with the fact that they went into Crimea. Well, Crimea had been part of Russia for 500 years. It was kind of a historic anomaly that it no longer was. They have been supporting the revolt in the Donbass area, which is right on the Russian border. You can look at people from different people's perspective. If you look at the Donbass people, they say "hey look, we were loyal Ukrainians until the CIA and

MI6 staged a coup, overthrew the pro-Russian government in Kiev with Molotov cocktails and rifles killing police and so forth". The United States had no problem recognizing that it emerged from that coup. Even though we are so big… "oh we can't possibly recognize a coup". It took us one day to recognize what was clearly a coup. Not one of those people had gotten any votes from the people. They were simply a bunch of thugs who were out in the streets. So, you have this one area that is very heavily Russian and it is part of Kiev and they say "look, we don't recognize the coup. We recognize the old government." If you look at it from that standpoint, that is pretty rational. You know, they were sworn to the old government. Not to a bunch of fire-bombing thugs who happened to kill a bunch of people and raid the office and steal everything in sight. These are petty things from the American perspective. It doesn't matter a whit.

Westall:

So what is going on foreign policy then? It seems like a
rational person would not make these decisions that we
are with our foreign policy; that there are factions
within our government fighting. Because Trump did a
180 on all of these things. The things we are doing just
does not make sense. Unless we want to go to war? Do
we want world war 3? Because that is what we are
acting like.

Black:

I really worry. You know, the nation states are no
longer what they were 50 years ago. The nation states
used to make decisions based on the interest of their
people. Today you have the globalists. I heard estimates
that there are 80 to 100 mega billionaires, rulers of
various countries, that really rule the world. They come
together in Davos Switzerland every year. If you want a
ticket to the meeting, it costs one hundred thousand
pounds. Well that's a big chunk of money. But if you or
I send in our check, they say "were sorry, we are all

sold out. We don't have a place for you". They are not looking for people who represent the interest of nation states, the interest of ordinary people. They are looking for people who really are globalists who ultimately want to shatter the cohesion of nation states. They want to break up the religious, the ethic unity of nations. Basically create nations where there is no mass of people who can oppose the government. Then eventually wrap all those into a centrally government. We will all be ruled and we will not even know who rules it. We don't know who rules the globalists now. We can single out one here and there; George Soros has been especially prominent. You know, he is just one. He just happens to be more of a fellow who seeks the limelight than some of the others. Others are a little bit more resistant about being in the forefront.

Westall:

Well so now, what is going on with Trump then? Do you believe, based on this situation, it sounds like Trump does not have a choice. Like he is at the mercy of a lot of these people. They must have something more powerful on him that he feels that he has to do a 180. Because everything else he talks about, all of his rhetoric, he talks about bringing jobs back. Every time he gives a speech, he talks about how he is making his commitments, and doing this and making commitments. But on foreign policy he is doing the exactly opposite of what he said he was going to do. It is not consistent with his pattern of behavior.

Black:

You know, I hate to talk about him specifically, but with politicians in general who support this type of thing. Let me give you an example. On the southern border of the United States, the people have been desperate to seal that border for the last 40 years and they elect people who say "I am going to seal the border". Then immediately those people are the ones who ensure the boarder is never sealed. Why? Because you have ultra-wealthy drug cartels and I think frankly a lot of them are bribed. And I think if you look at

Saudi Arabia, Saudi Arabia is in a position to send its ambassador who has diplomatic immunity and he doesn't have to worry about what he does. He can go in and he can tell influential people, and I am not talking about the president, but influential key people, he can say "look you have an election coming up, what does it cost you. I can cover that. Now it's not legal, but if you tell me, I can make it show up and it won't be on the record. And you may need some money personally. Here, write a number here. Write a number. Good, we can double that. We will make that show up in a Swiss bank account. We will give you a number". This is a tremendous temptation to a lot of people. I have no doubt that Saudi Arabia has been blackmailing and bribing people for decades and decades. And, I don't target any particular people that I suspect of this. And I hope that nothing like this happens with the people who surround Donald Trump, but they are targets. People who are in power are going to be targeted by people who have vast sums of money. Whether it's the drug cartels, whether it's the arm merchants, whether it is

Saudi Arabia, or the other people who are in the oil market. But particularly the Saudis.

Westall:

So how does somebody have the ability to stand up to this? Because people wanted, they were excited about somebody coming in to office to actually stand up to that whole corruption machine; the globalists, the corruption machine. People thought he would do that. I understand that the politics could be so rough that you have to give and take, and maybe that's part of the process that's going on with Trump, I don't know. But how do you possibly, it seems like we are marching into world war 3? So how can somebody realistically have the courage to realistically stand up to that without them being shoved out of office and never getting there anyways?

Black:

Well, first of all I agree with you that there has to be some kind of flexibility. You often take office and you don't know certain facts that do have a bearing on things. But, I would tell you, from a life of studying foreign policy, that his position on Russian, on NATO, on Syria were all correct. Now, the United States is on an absolutely suicidal course with Syria. There are two factions in the Syrian war; there is the Syrian government that is run by Bashar al Assad and there are the terrorists. The people in Syria will tell you, if you talk about this group of terrorists or that group, they will get angry because they say they are all the same. "Don't tell me about ISIS, don't tell me about Al Qaeda, or these others. They are all the same. They may squabble amongst themselves, but they are all the same". So, we have to decide. Are we on the side of the legitimate dually elected government of Syria, which had greater women's rights, greater religious freedom than any Arab nation when this war began. Or, do we side with the terrorists who are backed by Turkey, Qatar, and Saudi Arabia; three of the most despicably, vile dictatorships on the face of the planet. Which way do you go?

Westall:

It seems like we made our decision. I don't think the vast citizens of this country would decide that if we had a choice.

Black:

No. If the people understood for one minute that we have entered an unwritten alliance with Al Qaeda, the same group that brought down the towers on 911. They would be flabbergasted.

Westall:

Didn't the CIA have a hand in creating Al Qaeda?

Black:

I can't tell you that specifically. I think they had a role in creating ISIS. I see ISIS as a tool of various nations.

Westall:

Yeah, because they just sprung up with all of these resources.

Black:

It's a disposable tool. If you look at what is happening in Damascus right now, the rebels invested in Damascus early in the war and gradually they are being squeezed out; the last vestiges. What have they done? The Saudi Arabians have ordered Ja Al Islam to attack ISIS. They have been allies all this time and all of a sudden the Saudis send down orders to start attacking ISIS. Why? Because President Trump has said "I am going to attack ISIS, I am going to defeat ISIS". So he goes to these various countries "I am going to defeat ISIS. I want to say that I have done that". We can defeat ISIS, but what about Al Qaeda. ISIS didn't kill 3000 Americans on 911, that was Al Qaeda. And, now we call them the opposition? Or we call them the rebels? CIA has them constantly changing their names so people can never quite…

Westall:

Yeah, you never know. They are just one big mob of bad people.

Black:

Yes, and one of the most successful things that the CIA has done in this war is that they have said "Look, instead of saying ok, this is one massive army, we are going to chop it up into little pieces to where you have all of these foreign sounding names." They are constantly changing. One day they have one name; the next day they have another name. There are a thousand different groups. They are all terrorists. They have one singular objective which is: bring down Syria and when you brought down Syria you execute 2 million Christians, you execute 2 million Alawites, who are known as friends of the Christians, you begin executing the Shiites, and then you go on to all the other minorities, including the moderate Sunni rebels. Keep in mind most of the Syrian army that is fighting this war consists of Sunni soldiers, members of the Syrian armed forces.

Westall:

So if our side wins [sarcasm], there will be millions of people slaughtered?

Black:

Yes, and Christians in particular. People need to understand this. I have developed a tremendous sympathy for all of them. Including the moderate Sunnis because they are human beings and you can relate to them. I think for people on our side, most of whom are Christians or whose friends are Christians, the idea of slaughtering 2 million Christians and having them beheaded and having the women and the little girls sold on slave markets. The little girls... Religion, under Sharia law, they are permitted to have full complete sexual relations with a 9-year-old child. And they do this massively. So is this really what we want? You know under President Assad, 51% of college graduates in Syria were women.

Westall:

So we are helping some of the worst regimes take down one of the best regimes in the Middle East that had the standards and ideals that we talk about, value... Why would we do that? What's our point? World War 3? Globalism? We need a central bank there; we need to take him down for that reason?

Black:

There are a lot of things at play, but one of the immediate triggers of the war was that Saudi Arabia had wanted to run an oil line across Syria into Turkey for many years. They were very frustrated and angry at the Syrians for not allowing it. In around 2010, Qatar, which is a satellite of Saudi Arabia, was asked to run a major gas line. Qatar is essentially a gas field with a couple of hotels. And Syria did not give them permission to run the gas line. Within days, Qatar and Saudi Arabia begun pouring money into these faux rebel organizations. They weren't real, they were... you know, you had deserters from the army, people who

thought "ok, the United States is going to collapse the
government and I want to be on the winning side. I am
going to get something out of it". But you had Saudi
Arabia and Qatar pouring money in. Then you had
Turkey. Turkey has always cast a greedy eye on
Aleppo. Aleppo is the industrial center of Syria.
Turkey, keep in mind, Turkey is where all of the
terrorists flow into Syria. Almost all, now some come
in from Jordan, but the vast number come in through
Turkey. Turkey was the principle alley of ISIS for
about 5 years. Now it looks like ISIS has sort of run its
course and now they are going to be thrown away
[sarcasm]. After they have devoted their lives to this
mystical caliphate. I have spoken to witnesses who
stood at super highways going from Syria into Turkey
and they have said there were hundreds of oil tankers
bringing stolen oil into Syria into Turkey. And I asked
the questions, I said "hundreds in what period of
time?". And they said "hundreds everyday". And I said,
"Are they checked at the border". "[No] They are all
waved right through the border". At one point, there

was a fleet of 2 thousand oil tankers that was run by ISIS that was being sent directly to Turkey where Turkey was making a huge profit on it. The U.S. coalition never never interfered with this trafficking. When Russia sent its fairly modest expeditionary force, after several weeks they went in and they destroyed 500 oil tankers in a single day. The ISIS oil people became so complacent. They knew the U.S. coalition was never going to touch them. Then all of a sudden Russia came in and they were slaughtered.

Westall:

Yeah, they just said enough. It made Russia look like a hero.

Black:

Well, and you know, it's a very interesting thing. People always say well, Russia is communist, Russia is the Soviet Union. The Soviet Union died with the collapse of the wall and Russia has emerge a totally new country. One of the things very few people

recognize, in the Soviet Union, if you practice
Christianity, you could end up dead or sent to Siberia.
Christianity is highly encouraged in Russia today. More
so than it is in the United States. They actually have
military medals that are named after the saints. So this
is not the Russia that we were taught to believe in.
NATO wants us to continue to believe that the Soviet
Union exists, but the Soviet Union is gone.

Westall:
So why do we keep wanting to perpetuate the cold war
era ideals? What is the benefit? Is it the weapon
dealers? What is it?

Black:
You know, at the end of the cold war you had two great
alliances; One, the Soviet alliance, and one, the
American alliance, which was NATO. The Soviet
Union dissolved. Their defensive alliance dissolved. At
that point, we should have held a great march and
ceremony and pinned a medal on every soldier's

uniform and said "Good work, you've done well, we are sending you home". But we didn't. We kept NATO there and NATO, now that there was a total vacuum on the former Soviet side, all of the bureaucrats in NATO had to find a reason to exist. If you do that, you have to have an enemy. You can't have an alliance without an enemy. And so they began to paint Russia as being a whole lot like the Soviet Union, and it's not. And so they began to move constantly in violation of our agreements with the Soviet Union. Now we are routinely adding more and more countries to NATO. We are easing ourselves up on the Russian border. In fact, we are going into the Black Sea with war ships. We go right up to their territorial waters. And then they send in a jet to swoop in and warn us off. Then they say, "this is a provocative action of Russia". Well, this isn't a provocative action on their part, it's a provocative action on our part!

Westall:

So, at what point do you think Russia will say "this is enough" and that they will actually act? Or do you think they won't?

Black:

Well, I don't think they will for a certain time. But if we continue the march that we are on right now, at some point we are there and this group of global oligarchs is going to say "we are going to disassemble Russia". And the next thing, we are going to enter into a military conflict with Russia. I think I understand how President Putin thinks. I remember when Russia fought the war in Chechnya, after several failed attempts, they finally captured Grozny. Once he took firm control of it, now immediately afterwards, there were snipers in the city and this sort of thing, he flew himself in. He was wearing gym shorts and a t-shirt and he went jogging around the main streets of Grozny. Literally there were still buildings smoldering. And, I thought, this is not a guy who was in it for what he can get out of it. This is an extremely courageous guy. Whether people like it or not, he's a gutsy guy. You don't go jogging in Grozny right after it's been captured if you are not prepared to get shot. He did this. He is very much a patriot. And I will tell you what, if we push to the point where we invade Russia, which could happen at the rate we are going, he is the kind of guy which might very well say, "if they are going to destroy Russia, we are all going down in a ball of flame".

Westall:

They would rather go down then have us take them over?

Black:

I believe that is the case. I was a forward air controller and I fought with the first marine regime regimen on the ground in Vietnam. I was never going to be captured alive. I used to go deep into enemy territory, sometimes with very small patrols. And I had decided that if we ever get cornered, we only had so much ammunition, they outnumbered us by thousands, this was not going to be clustered last stand. The final order that I would give over the air would be "I want you to drop napalm and we are going to pop smoke and you drop it right on our position and we are all going down together. We are all going to die". And I honestly believe that he has that same mentality. He is very rational; he will make compromises where he needs to, but if we ever push him to the wall, we better not imagine that somehow he will roll over. This is not a Robert McNamara. This is not a Ted Kennedy. This is not one of these guys that says, "what's in it for me". This is a guy who is going to say "if I am the last president of Russia I am going to be the president that is going to say, you are not taking us down without going down yourselves".

Westall:

Do you think if that happens and we start to invade Russia, do you think the fight would come to our land? They clearly have the ability to do that.

Black:

Yes. Right now there are a lot more nuclear weapons that are active than there are ones operational ready to go. As near as I can tell, the United States and Russia each have about 1500 nuclear warheads of various sizes that are ready to go. You know, if the balloon goes up today, you can fire. The others are in various states of repair or disrepair. But if you have an exchange of 3000 nuclear weapons, and you never know if other countries get drawn into it. Israel has 600 nuclear weapons. Pakistan has... I don't know how many nuclear weapons. China has some. But, even if you just look at the United States and Russia. You are talking about a massive destruction of humanity. These are weapons that are far more than the weapons used at Nagasaki and Hiroshima. Some of them may be 100 times or even 200 times that force. You are going to see potentially the annihilation of the major portion of all of the human race on earth. And so, I really believe it is incumbent on the president to draw back from this and to say "look, the only vital security interest that the

United States has in Russia is avoiding a Nuclear war.
All of the other is trivial pursuit".

Westall:

Absolutely

Black:

How many people have you heard say, "oh my gosh,
you know what happened the other day? The Crimean's
voted to be part of Russia and that is hurting my cousin
and my brother and I am going to lose my job
because..." Why, it doesn't affect anybody.

Westall:

Exactly, it makes no sense.

Black:

No effect what so ever on the United States. It's purely
a construct of NATO and these global oligarchs who
benefit from the sales of weapons, manipulating the oil
markets, the sale of drugs, and major drug traffic. We

better stop it. You know its shows like yours where people get to hear what is really going on. It's really stunning… I had my doubts about Wikileaks when they first came out, but then I started reading what they were publishing. And I thought, my gosh, if it weren't for Wikileaks, none of us would have a clue as to what was happening.

Westall:

It is so important the stuff they are doing. And now there is a formal arrest warrant apparently. The United States is trying to step up its attack on Wikileaks.

Black:

And it emanates from the CIA you see. And the CIA, one of their jobs, is when we go to war, they are the ones who lay in place the rational for war. And it happened before the CIA. When I was a little boy, children knew that when the battle ship Maine was sunk in Havana Harbor by the Spanish allegedly. The Spanish who were still using sail ships, wooden hull sail ships, where you ram the cannon balls down. And here they have a modern battleship, and they decide to sink it? Children understood there was no motive. And now Americans have been so indoctrinated, we don't understand. Any time there is an allegation you have to look for a motive. This is what attorneys do. If you go to law school, you would be taught, look for the motive. Establish the motive, lay that out for the jury. Then you can prove your case. There was no motive to sink the Maine. It was an automatic destruction of the Spanish empire. Why would they do it? They wouldn't do it. And it didn't happen. You can go all through our history, but now the CIA is formally the go to people to say that "Saddam Hussein of Iraq had sarin gas". We really like sarin gas by the way. Sarin gas seems spooky and people seem to really glob onto it, so we use it all the time. Colin Powel, when he went up to the United Nations, he held a little test tube and he is talking about "Iraq has sarin gas, and this much sarin gas can destroy so much...". Well it was a farce. They had no sarin gas.

And we went in and killed over one hundred thousand Iraqis.

Westall:

I know, that is just unbelievable.

Black:

It is. Do you know that this is the 27th anniversary of when the United States had begun attacking Iraq? We have dropped 1/3 of a million bombs over the span of 27 years. For what? A country that never attacked us, never took any aggressive actions, never harbored terrorists. And here we are, there is no end in sight.

Westall:

But you know there is a cost more than people are realizing. I did a show a while ago about the suicides going on in our military. According to government numbers we have 22 people a day, veterans that are killing themselves.

People in the inner circles think it is actually higher.
You know, government numbers are not usually
accurate. But, according to government numbers we
have already surpassed, in one decade, which you know
has been going on for a long time, surpassed Vietnam

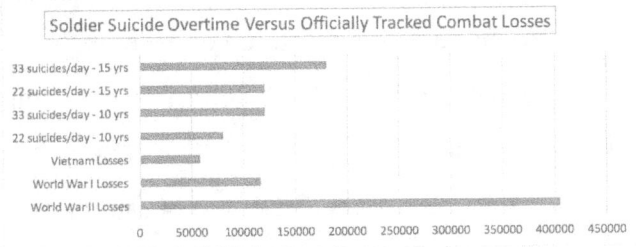

war losses with veteran suicides. I charted this all out.
Looking at 15 years' worth, we are already passing
world war one losses. People who died in military
combat during the Vietnam war or who have died in
military combat during world war one, we have
surpassed that when you count the number of suicides.
People do not realize how much it is effecting our
people. War has consequences.

Black:

Oh it does. I remember many years ago when we were talking about adopting the all-volunteer forces. I was on active duty and I really wanted it. I wanted to professionalize, and so forth. And I always remember what Charlie Rangel of New York, democrat liberal of New York, and he said, "we need to keep the draft because it gives us this loop, this feedback loop." You send people over and they say "wow, this is really stupid". And when they come back, and because they are not professional and they are not silenced, all of a sudden they become very vocal. I have been a little bit haunted by that. The moment he said it, I knew it was true, but I really wanted the all-volunteer armed force. I look back now and I wonder, how long ago would we have wrapped up things?

Westall:

It's so important

Black:

Do you know that the French fought for 8 years in
Algeria until finally it just got to be too much and they
had to pull out. It was because the people basically said,
"enough, we just can't fight forever". We have been
fighting in Afghanistan since 2001. That is twice as
long as the French had fought in Algeria. You know
with absolute certainty that the day we pull out the
government collapses because we fund something like
96% of the entire government. All of their public
works, all of their civil servants, all of their military is
all American funded. It's a façade. At a certain point,
ok "we don't like the way their culture is, we don't like
the way they treat women, the way they treat minority
religions, but it is not our country". At some point we
have to say that we are bankrupting ourselves doing this
and we are we are bankruptcy ourselves all over the
world.

Westall:

And you know as well as I do that the best way to get

someone to change is to bypass them cultural and just thrive while they aren't because they are acting this way. Whenever you have oppression in mass amounts in a culture, the whole country is going to be held back. So, if we can thrive, they will want part of that. The younger generations, people will want part of that. As long as there is freedom and free trade and things. But we, with what we are doing, we are not thriving because we are bankrupting ourselves and we are doing things to our armed services, we are doing all of these things. We are hurting ourselves to a level that we will have decades of ramifications.

Black:

Well, it really is. It has hurt this country very much. We have been in a perpetual state of war. In the first world war, they use to say, "this is the war to end all wars". Then at the end of the second world war, "Peace, we have peace". Now, no one talks about peace. No one talks about the end of the war. They have come up with this phrase "the long war". Which means it's never their intention to end this war.

Westall:

That's why we need the draft. Nobody wants it. Nobody wants the draft. The hurdle to bring the draft will be so hard, but that is the only thing that will end the war.

Black:

It would end the war. I am not necessary advocating the draft. There are so many difficulties. I am just saying that I know now that we made a very grave mistake when we did away with it. We weren't nearly as disciplined, we weren't nearly as orderly, but we had young kids who could come back and walk down the street and people would say "hey, what is happening in Afghanistan?", and they would say, "you wouldn't believe how stupid we are over there and we are fighting for nothing", and here we send highly discipline professionals, their families, their careers are at stake. But they are saying the same things privately.

Westall:

Yes, they are. So, I am going to ask a sad question, does the human race need a big war every so often to cleanse itself emotionally and to start over? It's a terrible question, it's a terrible thing to think about, but is it true?

Black:

[Sigh]

Westall:

Sorry, I kind of put you on the spot.

Black:

I don't think so... You know, we would be completely cleansed by now if that was the case. We have been at war for so many years. You go back to the year 2001, there hasn't been a time that we haven't been at war. I

was reading about Iran, and of course, they have their
problems, don't get me wrong, but they have never
been expansionists, and the things we call terrorism...
well when we went into Iraq, which is right next door to
them, sure they funneled weapons over and they tried to
do what they could to kick us out. Why? Because they
were next. If China came into Mexico do you think we
would not be supplying weapons to the Mexican
revolutionaries? Of course. They keep repeating this
thing "Iran is the major source of terrorism", and I ask,
"give me an example", and they say, "you know,
decades ago they were involved in the bombing of the
marine barracks in Lebanon", and I say, "ok, alright,
maybe they were...". Look, I was a marine, I love the
service people, I hate to see them hurt. But the question
would be "what were we doing with Marines in
Lebanon? What business did we have with Marines in
Lebanon?". I think if you look at Iran over the last
thousand years, their foreign policy has been: keep
people away from us, keep them from getting to our
borders. But they are not trying to enlarge the country,

not like Turkey. Turkey is trying to enlarge, sever off
people from this country. Now they are starting to make
noises that they think they should have more of Greece
than they got in the treaty of 1923. They are our allies.
The people who are expansionists, who are aggressive,
who are nasty dictators. Iran, are they trying to get
weapons? Maybe they are, but I don't think they are
trying to take over the world. I feel much more
threatened by Turkey today and by Saudi Arabia today
than I do by Russia or Iran today. Because Saudi Arabia
is planting Wahhabism all around the globe.
Wahhabism is the most fundamental, vicious form of
Islam. There are a lot of places where Islam is practice
and, you know, people get along, but they are
radicalizing people all over the world. Then you look at
Turkey. They just did a referendum that has made
Turkey the new Hitler. He has absolute power over
everything. He can appoint the majority of their high
court. He can decide who can run for parliament. He
can dissolve all of parliament if he wants. He can
declare a state of emergency and nobody has any

oversight. The other day he just threw a thousand people in jail because they were known to have liked Gulen, who is a Turkish fellow who is now living up in Pennsylvania. Because they liked him, "well put them in jail. Let them rot away in jail". This man is the modern day Hitler and he is the greatest danger to Western civilization. But he is our good ally.

Westall:
Yeah, he is our good ally and we are fighting with him [sarcasm]

Black:
Well, we are committed by treaty under NATO if he feels attacked. American kids are supposed to go out and fight for these stinkers under this dictator. It wasn't but 3 or 4 years ago where U.S. Navy ships were pulling into port in Turkey and Turkish gangs were running them down and beating them up in town because they were Christians and because they were Americans. Didn't get front page of the New York

Times, but it was widely published. These are the people that we are allied with. Nobody was ever running around beating up Americans in Syria. Syria was one of the five safest nations on earth before we decided we were going to over throw them.

Westall:

We took something great and we decided to do something...

Black:

You know, I am beyond the point where I am interested in solving everybody's problem all around the globe. There are people who are mistreated and there's corruption out there. We often say "oh, such and such is corrupt". Are we not a corrupt country?

Westall:

Yes, well that's why it bothers me that we would go to war. As awful as it was, the 80 people that died when they claimed the Syrians gassed their own people, as awful as that is, the fact that we would use that as a basis to go to war, well we were already at war, makes no sense to me when there are thousands of people dying all over the place for all sorts of nefarious reasons.

Black:

A week after that, there had been an agreement between the Syrian government and the Qatari government representing all of the terrorists. The terrorists had besieged a pro-government area and the Syrian government had a rebel area under siege. They agreed to a swap and they brought commercial buses to each place. The Syrian government has a pristine record of always observing these treaties scrupulously. When they are talking about exchanges driving these buses. On the other hand, the terrorists murdered 126 people, including many many children by putting IEDs where they knew they were going to kill helpless, disarmed civilians and it didn't even make the front pages of the newspapers. They killed more people than died at Ka

Sukoon the week before. [sarcasm] And ah... what the heck, it's just Syrian people. It's not terrorists, we love the terrorist, the terrorists are our guys. [end sarcasm] We are totally allied with Al Qaeda, the group that brought down the twin towers. The United States has been on their side as their allied ever since around 2010, 2011 and it's bizarre. It is suicidal. It's bankrupting the nation. It's corrupting us. It's morally so decadent the idea that we would be on the side of the people that brought about the death of more Americans in an attack on the American mainland than any other time in the history of the United States.

Westall:

With you being so close to Washington D.C., you're a state senator in Virginia, how much influence do you have? It's a unique position being so close to Washington D.C. Do you get involved in any of those, that kind of politics for foreign policy? Do you have access to that now?

Black:

Yes, in a couple of different ways. One is that I am a fairly respected voice in foreign affairs. And so I am able to articulate things in a way that people can understand them. I have studied enough to where I have a very clear picture to what is going on in certain areas. You know, I get invited to different embassies. I have spent time at the Pakistani embassy. When President El Sisi of Egypt came, I addressed members of parliament from that delegation. I am a great fan of President El Sisi. I think he is pushing the envelope as far as he can reasonably do in that country. I keep up a lot of relations with people who are in the Middle East and I just think to perhaps just give hope to people. There are a number of people who are antiwar for very good reasons, but there are very few people who have experienced extremely bitter fierce fighting like I have who are saying what we are doing is wrong. It brings a certain air of credibility to it. Obviously, I am constantly putting my position as Senator on the line because there are people who disagree with it. And that is just the way it is. To me, I have a picture; there is a briefing that I give, and the last slide I bring up is a photograph that was taken at a Christian Cathedral in Damascus. There is a school beside it. They brought together all of the children; they are teenagers, older teenagers. We all took a picture together. They all just have a look, sort of a glow of youthful happiness about them. I usually close by saying "a lot of people ask you, you don't have any relatives in Syria, why are you so passionate about it?", and I say, "if you look at the faces of the people on this slide, if the United States succeeds in toppling Syria, in the next 2 years, all of those people will be dead. All of the children will be dead. Some of them will be sex slaves. The children will be raped. All of them will be destroyed". This is why I am so passionate about it and I am willing to risk everything.

Westall:

You are estimating about 4 million people?

Black:

Yes, 2 million Christians, 2 million Alawites. There would be others also. There would be the Sunni Muslims who have cooperated with the government. Many of them would die. This would be one of the biggest bloodlettings in history. It would not happen without the United States being actively involved. We now train terrorists in Jordan, Saudi Arabia, Qatar, and Turkey. We arm them, we pay the salaries of some of them, then we send them across the Syrian border where they go and rape, and murder, and annihilate Christian villages. This is being done under a CIA program known as "Timber Sycamore", it was highly classified. Thanks to our good friends at Wikileaks, we know about it. I just recently found out the name of it. I knew it existed because I had put together pieces of it over 6 years. When the Russians sent their expeditionary force in, the Syrian army immediately began rolling back the terrorists. If the United States had not rushed tow anti-tank missiles to all of the terrorists; to Al Qaeda, to ISIS, all of these different terrorist groups, that war would have been over by now. Refugees would be returning. The nation would be rebuilding. There would be joy, there would be happiness. People would be rebuilding their lives. But, we made a decision in the White House to rush tow anti-tank missiles which blunted the force of the Syrian attack. And we are still doing it. We could still end that war with a decision of the president. If the president sent out a memo, "By virtue of this executive order, any person who assists any rebel group in Syria will be terminated immediately. Every organization will work to assist the Syrian government in restoring its integrity and in defeating all rebel groups. No matter what their designation, without specific exceptions granted by the White House." We would end that war in no time at all.

Westall:

That's why I was wondering what courage needed to be… or who's putting the pick into Trump's side and changing… There is an internal debate and struggle going on that caused him to take a 180.

Black:

The foreign policy conservatives are being purged and it began with Michael Flynn. Michael Flynn was perhaps the most important member of the entire cabinet. He knew where all the skeletons were buried. He knew right from wrong. He knew how to end the war. He was purged. They came up with some concoction to get rid of him. Now, just one by one. Katie McFarland went and then you know, a whole variety of them are being pushed out of influential positions. In their place, neocons who have run this war for decades. I wish every neocon had to go to Walter Reed hospital like I do, and see young, strong and vibrant guys with their legs missing up to their hips. Being strolled around, their entire lives destroyed. Then I would like to say, "your children are going to be put in the front lines of the infantry. They are going to be making patrols in Afghanistan. If you like it so much, your kids, your daughters. They are going to go anonymously, no one will know it's a senator, it's a congressman, it's a white house official. They are going to go. Just be aware that you may have to care for them for the rest of their lives because they may come back without legs, without arms, blinded, burned to a crisp to where their whole life they have to get an operation each month because their skin is tightening up". If they understood the real price, but instead they rake in money.

Westall:

And the real price mentally too. The fact that we are having so many soldiers die from killing themselves. And for every soldier that doesn't commit suicide, the torture that they have inside to being able to mentally deal with what they had to do and witness.

Black:

You know, I look back at Vietnam. I have no regrets. But I tell you, if someone told me, you have to attack Syria, I would carry that to the grave with me. Because I would know that I would be killing innocent people to benefit the most vial, evil, satanic people on the globe. That would bother me.

Westall:

And I think that is what is going on. I think that's why there are so many people just really struggling. So how can people learn more about you, reach you, and support you? You are such a refreshing voice out there that is telling and sharing the truth and getting this stuff out there and educating people. People need to understand what is really going on. Where our tax dollars are going and what the ramifications are.

Black:

The easiest way is to go to SenatorBlack.com. Just look that up. You will get my website. That will link you up to everything that we send out on Twitter, on Facebook, and you can sign up for Facebook, you can sign up for Twitter. Usually we try to make our Facebook more of a local thing for when we campaign. But the Twitter, we have Twitter all over the world. We have tens of thousands of people on Twitter. But they want to because, I tell you, if you read the main stream media, you do not have a clue what the truth is. Not the faintest end of what the truth is.

Westall:

That is exactly right. And that is not a good commentary. We need to change that in order for our country to move forward. Thank you so much for joining us today and thank you so much for your service to our country and everything that you do.

Black:

Thank you so much. I have enjoyed being with you. I appreciate being with you. It's the alternative media, it's the internet. This is the only way we are able to compete and surprisingly we do a pretty good job of it.

SYRIA STRONGHOLDS

May 10th report from Al Jazeera:

After years of civil war, Syria is now a country that lies in ruins. Thousands of people have died, millions have fled.

With no end of the war in sight, groups continue to battle for control over large parts of the country.

The Syrian government, ISIL, Kurdish factions, and several other rebel groups are still fighting for some of the most important parts of the country.

Government troops, supported by Russian war planes, have gained some ground over the past few months, expelling ISIL from Palmyra and other important places.

At the end of 2016, the Syrian government managed to capture Aleppo, one of the main battlegrounds in the conflict.

Meanwhile Kurdish fighters have made gains in the northern part of Syria, reducing the territory under control by ISIL.

Turkish troops recently joined the fight against ISIL, expelling the group from the city of Jarablus.ISIL has not only been losing territory in Syria, but, as this map shows, also in Iraq, where the Kurds and the Iraqi Security Forces are slowly making their way to ISIL's last stronghold, Mosul.

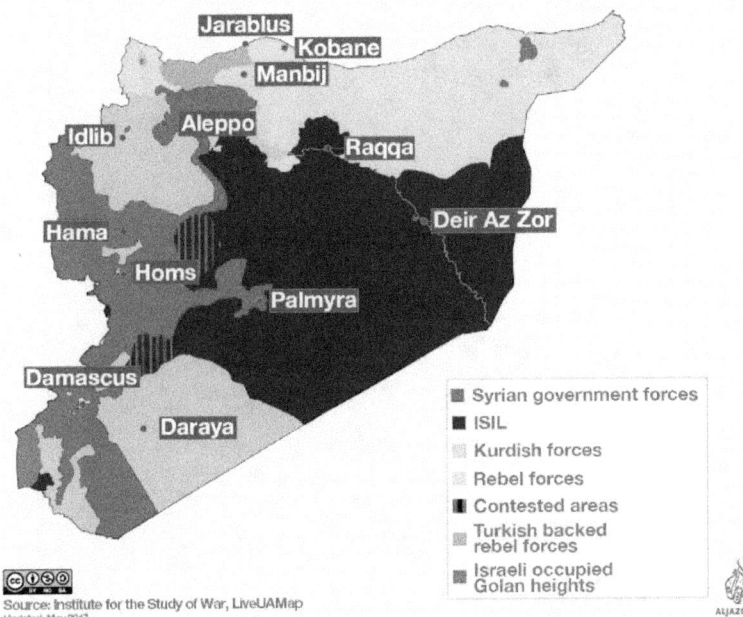

Syria: Who controls what?

Jarablus
Kobane
Manbij
Idlib
Aleppo
Raqqa
Hama
Deir Az Zor
Homs
Palmyra
Damascus
Daraya

- Syrian government forces
- ISIL
- Kurdish forces
- Rebel forces
- Contested areas
- Turkish backed rebel forces
- Israeli occupied Golan heights

Source: Institute for the Study of War, LiveUAMap
Updated: May 2017

ALJAZEERA

BIOGRAPHY: SARAH WESTALL

Sarah Westall is a successful entrepreneur and business executive. In the past 25 years, she has created and developed multiple companies including a successful  management and consulting firm and a multi-million-dollar international import and manufacturing company. She has a dynamic leadership career spent building high-performance teams in highly competitive industries. She has an entrepreneurial attitude, energy, and style.

She has proven ability to define company positioning by driving the development and execution of innovation, market entry plays, long-term growth, strategy, business development and strategic initiatives.

Sarah has a computer science and business management systems degree from the College of Science and Engineering at the University of Minnesota with an emphasis in Management Information Systems from the Carlson Business School.

Sarah started her career at the center of the Internet revolution at US West communications where she was promoted multiple times to eventually become director of the advanced networking group responsible for all of the systems design and development for !NTERPRISE, the Internet and Networking arm of US West. At the time, the company captured 75% of the frame relay market, the backbone of the Internet. They also engaged in partnerships with Microsoft, NeXT, Time Warner, and other leaders in the fast growing telecommunications industry in the early 90's.

Later, Sarah left the corporate world and started her own enterprise. While starting her business she also attended the University of Colorado working towards her MBA. After completing most of the coursework, her business, Ichor Corporation exploded, forcing her to switch focus and invest all of her energies in managing the fast growth multi-million-dollar business.

Currently, Sarah is a partner at Galex Consulting, an adjunct at the University of Minnesota's top rated Carlson business school teaching classes in leadership, ethics, management, and entrepreneurship, and the host of the national radio show, "Business Game Changers". Her national radio show features leaders in Business, Government, Society, and Science. Her significant experience and knowledge in technology, systems engineering, business, and entrepreneurship provides insight and depth unparalleled in the media.

You can see over 200 episodes and articles at SarahWestall.com

BIOGRAPHY: SENATOR BLACK

Senator Richard Black is currently a Republican member of the Virginia State Senate and is the most vocal politician in the country against the Syrian conflict. His experiences in the military provide him a unique perspective to intelligently speak on the realities of the region.

Black was a career military officer. He served in both
the U.S. Marines and in the U.S. Army JAG Corps. He
served a total of 31 years active and reserve, rising from
the rank of private to full colonel. Later he served as the
Chief of the Army's Criminal Law Division at the
Pentagon focusing on Africa and the Middle East.

In April 2014, Black sent a letter to Assad thanking
"the Syrian Arab Army for its heroic rescue
of Christians in the Qalamoun Mountain Range",
praising Assad for "treating with respect all Christians
and the small community of Jews in Damascus," and
stating it was obvious that the rebel side of the war was
largely being fought by "vicious war criminals linked to
Al Qaeda"

On April 27, 2016, Black began a three-day trip to
Syria in support of its government. Explaining his trip
in a series of Twitter exchanges with the Washington
Post, Black wrote that the U.S. was "allied with two of
the most vile nations on earth, Saudi Arabia and

Turkey, which are intent on imposing a [Wahhabi] fundamentalist government on the Syrian people." The Islamic State has included Black in a list of its enemies, calling him "The American Crusader".

Senator Black has been vocal on the ramifications if Syria falls; We will have mass slaughter... "Over 4 million Christians, Jews, moderate rebels, and others will be slaughtered... It will be one of the worst blood baths in human history".

You can learn more about Senator Richard Black at SenatorBlack.com

www.ingramcontent.com/pod-product-compliance
Lightning Source LLC
Chambersburg PA
CBHW062039280526
45788CB00003B/1039